PLAYTALES

HANSEL & GRETEL

MOIRA BUTTERFIELD

Heinemann Interactive Library
Des Plaines, Illinois

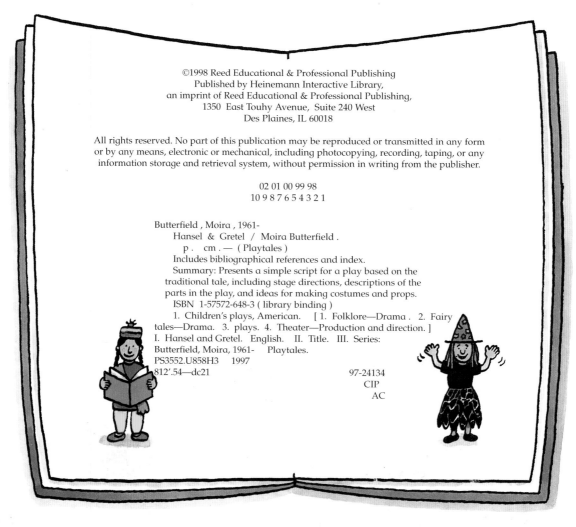
Butterfield , Moira , 1961-
    Hansel & Gretel / Moira Butterfield .
       p . cm . — (Playtales)
    Includes bibliographical references and index.
    Summary: Presents a simple script for a play based on the
traditional tale, including stage directions, descriptions of the
parts in the play, and ideas for making costumes and props.
    ISBN 1-57572-648-3 (library binding)
    1. Children's plays, American.   [1. Folklore—Drama . 2. Fairy
tales—Drama. 3. plays. 4. Theater—Production and direction.]
I. Hansel and Gretel. English. II. Title. III. Series:
Butterfield, Moira, 1961-   Playtales.
PS3552.U858H3   1997
812'.54—dc21
                                    97-24134
                                       CIP
                                       AC

Editor: David Riley • Art Director: Cathy Tincknell • Designer: Anne Sharples
Photography: Trever Clifford • Illustrator: Frances Cony • Props: Anne Sharples

Thanks to: Peter Sanders, Natalie Walsh, Yasmina Kahouadji and Shaka Omwony

Printed and bound in Italy

You will need to use scissors and glue to make the props for
your play. Always make sure an adult is there to help you.

Use only water-based face paints and makeup. Children with
sensitive skin should use makeup and face paints with caution.

Contents

4 • Choose a Part
5 • Reading the Play
6 • Things to Make
9 • Stage and Sounds
10 • The Play

THE STORY OF HANSEL AND GRETEL

Hansel and Gretel find themselves in big trouble when a wicked witch comes into their lives. Hansel almost becomes the witch's supper, but the children find a way to save themselves just in time and they turn the tables on the horrible hag.

❧ Choose a Part ❧

This play is a story that you can read with your friends and perhaps even act out in front of an audience. You need up to five people. Before you start, choose which parts you would like to play.

Hansel
A brave and clever little boy.

Storyteller
Someone who helps tell the tale.

Witch
A wicked woman who starts off disguised as a stepmother and an old lady.

Gretel
A brave and clever little girl.

Woodcutter
A poor man under a wicked spell.

How many people are going to take part?

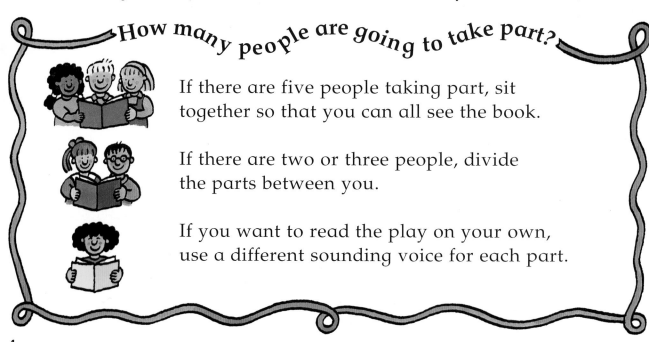

If there are five people taking part, sit together so that you can all see the book.

If there are two or three people, divide the parts between you.

If you want to read the play on your own, use a different sounding voice for each part.

Reading the Play

Hansel　　**Gretel**　　**Witch**　　**Storyteller**　**Woodcutter**

The play is made up of different lines. Next to each line there is a name and a picture. This shows who should be talking.

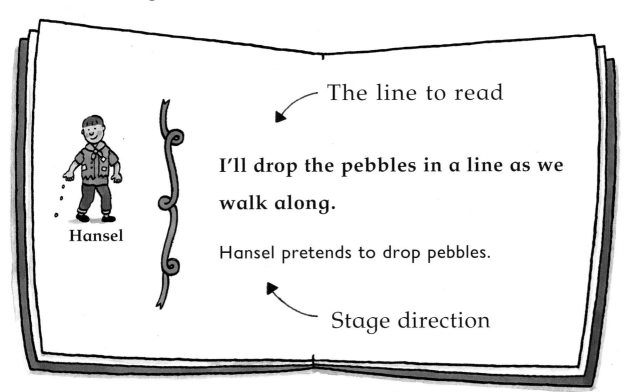

The line to read

I'll drop the pebbles in a line as we walk along.

Hansel pretends to drop pebbles.

Stage direction

Hansel

In between the lines, there are some stage directions. They are suggestions for things you might do, such as, making a noise or acting something out.

Things to Make

Here are some suggestions for costumes.

THE WITCH: CLOTHES AND PROPS

The Witch begins as a stepmother and old lady. She should wear a black top, pipe cleaner glasses, a black skirt, and an apron. When she becomes the Witch, she should take off the apron and put on a witch's hat.

Make a Witch Hat
You need:

- Rectangle of stiff blue paper, 20 in. by 36 in.
- Larger piece of matching paper
- Scissors, glue, and pencil
- Tape and paint

1. Lay the paper rectangle on a flat surface. Starting at the bottom right-hand corner, roll it up into a cone.

2. Hold the cone together and fit it on your head. Adjust it if you need to, and then tape the loose edges inside and out.

3. Trim around the bottom of the cone to make a straight edge.

4. Stand the cone on the second piece of paper and trace a circle around it. Draw a second, wider circle around that, and cut it out.

5. Cut lines out from the middle to the inner circle to make points. Bend them up, and glue or tape them snugly inside the cone.

If you like, paint magic stars onto your hat and tape a fringe of ragged black paper around the inside of the cone to make witch hair.

Make a Black Skirt

You need:

- A black trash bag
- Scissors
- Enough string or black ribbon to tie around your waist in a bow

1. Snip raggedly along the bottom edge of the bag to open it up.

2. Cut some small slits round the top of the bag and thread the string or ribbon through. Pull it tightly and tie it around your waist.

HANSEL, GRETEL, AND THE WOODCUTTER: CLOTHES AND PROPS

Hansel and his father should wear jeans or pants and a T-shirt or shirt. Gretel should wear a skirt and a T-shirt or blouse. Hansel could wear a scarf around his neck, and Gretel could wear one around her hair. To show they are poor, they could have worn-out sneakers and ragged peasant vests.

Make a Ragged Vest

You need:

- Stiff paper
- Scissors, pencil, and ruler
- Tape or glue
- A T-shirt that fits you

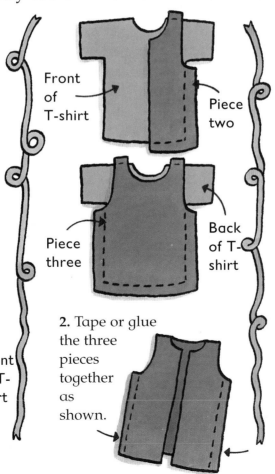

Front of T-shirt

Piece two

Piece three

Back of T-shirt

1. You need to cut three pieces out to make your vest. Use your T-shirt as a pattern.

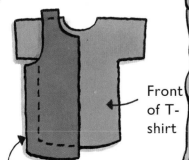

Front of T-shirt

Piece one

2. Tape or glue the three pieces together as shown.

3. Cut around the edges to make the vest ragged. If you like, paint a patch on the vest, or stick one on made of paper.

7

PROPS: CARD CAGE, CHICKEN BONE, KEY AND BOX

Make a Cardboard Cage
You need:
- Large rectangle of cardboard (you could use part of an empty cardboard box)
- Ruler, pencil, and scissors
- Paint

1. Use your ruler and pencil to draw some bars inside the rectangle.

2. Cut around the bars so you can peer through them. Paint the cage front gray with a black keyhole.

When Hansel is in the cage, he should hold up the cardboard cage in front of his face.

Key and Box
Find a small cardboard box (such as an empty food package), and paint over any decoration on it. This is the box the Witch will use to hide jewels and the key to the cage.

If you like, roll up some pieces of shiny aluminum foil to make jewels for the box.

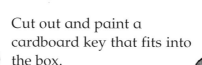

Cut out and paint a cardboard key that fits into the box.

Chicken Bone
Use a clean dry stick to represent a chicken bone.

Pipe cleaner Glasses
Bend five pipe cleaners and twist them together as shown:

Face Painting Ideas
Give the Witch a green face, a black wart, and black eyebrows.

Give the children smudged cheeks to make them look like they've been lost in the woods.

Stage and Sounds

Once you have read the play through, you may want to perform it in front of an audience. If so, read through this section first. It has been kept very simple. You may want to add some extra performance ideas of your own in rehearsal.

COSTUME CHANGES

The Witch needs to alter her costume once. The stage directions tell you when to do this. Keep the witch hat offstage and out of sight, perhaps behind a table covered with a tablecloth or on a table hidden behind an open door.

PROPS

Keep the props out of sight behind a table or an open door. Make sure you can get to them easily though.

SOUNDS

Forest noises:

When the children are in the woods, make noises like screeching owls and howling wolves. You could get an assistant to do this offstage.

LIGHTING

You could do a really exciting performance at night with the room light on and flashlights ready. Get an assistant to switch the room light off when the children are stuck in the forest at night. The actors should then read their parts using flashlights until the light goes on again. Make sure you rehearse this carefully so you can work out exactly when you want the light to go on and off.

REHEARSING

Rehearse the play before you ask someone to watch.

The Play

Storyteller

Once a poor widowed Woodcutter lived on the edge of a forest. He had a son named Hansel and a daughter named Gretel. One day he married a bad woman who was really a witch. She put her husband under a spell so he would do whatever she asked.

Stepmother (really the witch)

Woodcutter, we can't afford to feed these greedy children of yours. Tonight you must take them into the forest and leave them to find their own food.

Gretel: What shall we do?
We'll starve in the forest!

Hansel: Don't worry, Gretel. I have an idea. This afternoon I'll go out to play in the backyard and secretly fill my pockets with shiny pebbles.

Gretel: Then what?

Hansel: You'll see!

Hansel appears to fill his pockets with pebbles.

Woodcutter

Come on, children. I must take you deep into the forest.

Hansel

I'll drop the pebbles in a line as we walk along.

Woodcutter

While the children aren't looking, I'll slip away and leave them here.

Make some night time forest sounds such as an owl hooting.

12

Hansel

Look. The moon is shining on the line of pebbles I dropped. If we follow their trail, we'll get home.

Storyteller

When the children reached home, their wicked Stepmother was furious. She locked them upstairs with only stale bread and water for tea.

Gretel

I'm sure she will try to get rid of us again. I know! I'll hide some bread in my pockets.

Gretel appears to fill her pockets.

Woodcutter

Children, come. I must take you back into the forest.

Gretel

I'll drop a trail of breadcrumbs as we walk along. We'll be able to follow it back home again.

Hansel

That wicked woman will need to be more clever if she wants to get rid of us!

Gretel appears to drop breadcrumbs.

Storyteller

Poor children! Their wicked Stepmother was VERY clever. She put a spell on the birds in the forest and they hopped behind Hansel and Gretel eating up all the breadcrumbs!

Gretel

The trail of crumbs has disappeared and so has father!

Hansel

It's darker than ever tonight.

Make the noise of an owl hooting.

Help! We're lost!

Hansel and Gretel

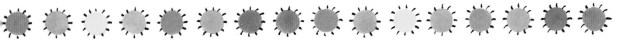

Storyteller

The children stumbled through the frightening forest until they came upon a strange little house. Be careful, children!

Hansel

The bricks look as if they are made of chocolate.

Gretel

I think the chimney is a cake!

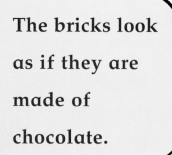

Hansel

Yum, yum! My favorite candies are stuck all over the front door. I'm sure it won't matter if I just eat one...

Hansel appears to pick off a candy and eat it.

Witch
(pretending to be old lady)

Hello, who's eating my house?

Hansel

Oh! I didn't know anyone was inside. I'm sorry.

Witch
(pretending to be old lady)

It doesn't matter, young man. Why are you two out in the dark? Come inside. You can sleep here tonight.

Be careful, little children! This kind old lady is really your wicked Stepmother, the WITCH!

Storyteller

Witch cackles.

17

COSTUME CHANGE

Witch takes off apron and glasses. Puts on witch hat.

> Wake up, wake up little boy!

Witch

> Is it morning? Who are you? Stop pushing me!

Hansel

> I'm your worst nightmare! In you go, into your cage!

Witch

Hansel holds the cage prop in front of his face.

> Help! Help!

Hansel

18

Gretel

What have you done with my brother?

Witch

I've locked him in a cage, and only I have the key. Hee, hee, hee! Now, you will do all the chores, little girl... Or your brother will suffer.

Gretel

You horrible witch! I'll never work for you!

Witch

Oh yes you will, madam. You can start by making a big breakfast for your little brother. I want to fatten him up.

Storyteller

The Witch had one weakness. She could not see without her glasses on. After a few days, Gretel noticed this. She hid them and told Hansel her secret plan. The next day the Witch went to check on Hansel...

Witch

Are you eating your food, boy? I want you plump as a pig so I can eat you! Let me feel your finger to see how fat you're getting.

Hansel hands the stick 'bone' through the cage for the witch to feel.

Hansel
(whispers)

I'll give her this chicken bone to feel. She can't see it's not my finger.

Witch

You're still too thin to eat, boy. We must feed you more. Gretel, bake some bread for your brother. Go and see if the oven is hot enough.

Gretel

I don't know how hot it should be. I've never baked bread before.

Witch

You stupid girl. You must open the oven door and put your head inside, like this...

The Witch appears to look behind a door. She shouts and pretends to fall into the oven, going offstage as she does this.

21

Storyteller

As quick as a flash, Gretel pushed the Witch into the hot oven and slammed the door.

Hansel

Quick, Gretel. Find the key to my cage!

Gretel

The Witch keeps it somewhere in this room. Let me see... I'll look in this box. Here it is. Wow! The box is filled with jewels, too!

If you like, use the box and key prop here. Pretend to unlock Hansel's cage with the key. Then put the cardboard cage down.

Storyteller

Hansel and Gretel filled their pockets with jewels and ran out of the Witch's house. She never escaped from her oven, and it served her right!

Hansel

How can we find our way home?

Gretel

Look, the birds are flying around us. I think they are trying to tell us something.

Storyteller

The birds were no longer under the Witch's spell and they were sorry they had eaten the breadcrumbs. They led the children back home.

Gretel

Father, father! We're home!

The children hold out the box of jewels.

Woodcutter

Look at all these jewels. We're rich!

Woodcutter

I am no longer under the Witch's spell. Do you think we shall live happily ever after?

Hansel and Gretel

Of course we will!

$19.92

DATE			